Judicial Writing Manual: A Pocket Guide for Judges

Second Edition

Federal Judicial Center
2013

This Federal Judicial Center publication was undertaken in furtherance of the Center's statutory mission to develop educational materials for the judicial branch. While the Center regards the content as responsible and valuable, this publication does not reflect policy or recommendations of the Board of the Federal Judicial Center.

first printing

Contents

Editor's Note v

Foreword to the First Edition vii

Foreword to the Second Edition ix

I. Introduction 1

II. Determining the Scope of the Opinion 3
    Three types of decisions 3
    Factors to consider 3
        Facts and issues 4
        Audience 5
        Publication 6

III. Preparing to Write the Opinion 9
    Developing outlines 9
    Using law clerks 10
    Reviewing materials 11

IV. Writing the Opinion 13
    Structure 13
    Introduction 13
    Statement of issues 14
    Statement of facts 15
    Discussion of legal principles 16
        Standard of review 16
        Order of discussion of issues 16
        Issues to address 17
        Alternative holdings 17
        Case citations 18
        Secondary sources 18
        Quotations 18
        Avoiding advocacy 19
        Treatment of the court below 19
    Disposition and instructions 19

V. Editing the Opinion 21
    Problems in judicial writing 21
        Wordiness 21
        Lack of precision and clarity 21
        Poor organization 21
        Cryptic analysis 22
        Pomposity and humor 22
    Guidelines for good writing 22
        Eliminate unnecessary words 22
        Be succinct and direct 23
        Use plain English 23
    Use of footnotes and citations 24
        Footnotes 24
        Citations 24
    Careful editing 25
        Reread and revise 25
        Put the draft aside and come back to it with a fresh perspective 26
        Ask a new reader to criticize a draft 26

VI. Writing Joint Opinions, Dissents, and Concurrences 27
    Joint opinions 27
    Commenting on a draft prepared by another judge 28
    Dissenting opinions 28
    Concurring opinions 30

VII. Reading About Writing 31
    Books 32
    Articles 32

Appendix A: Sample Memorandum Opinion 33

Appendix B: Sample Summary Order 35

Appendix C: Sample Standards of Review 37

Appendix D: Sample Dispositions 39

Appendix E: Sample Brief Dissenting Opinions 41

Appendix F: Sample Brief Concurring Opinions 43

Editor's Note

The Center prepared the first edition of the *Judicial Writing Manual* in 1991 under the guidance of the following Board of Editors:

- Alvin B. Rubin, *Chair*
  U.S. Circuit Judge
- Wilfred Feinberg
  U.S. Circuit Judge
- John C. Godbold
  U.S. Circuit Judge
  Director Emeritus, Federal Judicial Center
- James Dickson Phillips, Jr.
  U.S. Circuit Judge
- Louis H. Pollak
  U.S. District Judge
- William W Schwarzer
  U.S. District Judge
  Director Emeritus, Federal Judicial Center
- Clifford Wallace
  U.S. Circuit Judge
- Patricia M. Wald
  Chief U.S. Circuit Judge
- A. Leo Levin
  Professor, University of Pennsylvania
  Director Emeritus, Federal Judicial Center
- Paul J. Mishkin
  Professor, University of California, Berkeley
- Stephen J. Wermiel
  The Wall Street Journal

The Center and the Board of Editors were assisted in preparing the first edition by the following judges, who participated in telephone interviews to discuss their experience with and views on judicial writing: Ruggero J. Aldisert, Richard S. Arnold, Stephen Breyer, Frank M. Coffin, John J. Gibbons, Robert E. Ginsberg, Ruth Bader Ginsburg, Frank M. Johnson, Jr., Robert E. Keeton, Lloyd King, James K. Logan, Prentice H. Marshall, Monroe G. McKay, Richard A. Posner, Joseph T.

Sneed, Gerald B. Tjoflat, Jack B. Weinstein, and John Minor Wisdom. Their thoughtful responses contributed substantially to this manual.

Foreword to the First Edition

The link between courts and the public is the written word. With rare exceptions, it is through judicial opinions that courts communicate with litigants, lawyers, other courts, and the community. Whatever the court's statutory and constitutional status, the written word, in the end, is the source and the measure of the court's authority.

It is therefore not enough that a decision be correct—it must also be fair and reasonable and readily understood. The burden of the judicial opinion is to explain and to persuade and to satisfy the world that the decision is principled and sound. What the court says, and how it says it, is as important as what the court decides. It is important to the reader. But it is also important to the author because in the writing lies the test of the thinking that underlies it. "Good writing," Ambrose Bierce said, "essentially is clear thinking made visible." Ambrose Bierce, Write It Right 6 (rev. ed. 1986).

To serve the cause of good opinion writing, the Federal Judicial Center has prepared this manual. It is not held out as an authoritative pronouncement on good writing, a subject on which the literature abounds. Rather, it distills the experience and reflects the views of a group of experienced judges, vetted by a distinguished board of editors. No one of them would approach the task of writing an opinion, or describe the process, precisely as any of the others would. Yet, though this is a highly personal endeavor, some generally accepted principles of good opinion writing emerge and they are the subject of this manual.

We hope that judges and their law clerks will find this manual helpful and that it will advance the cause for which it has been prepared.

William W Schwarzer
Director Emeritus, Federal Judicial Center

Foreword to the Second Edition

More than twenty years have passed since the Federal Judicial Center published the first edition of this manual on judicial writing. In that relatively brief time, many of our basic assumptions about written communication have been challenged profoundly by technological change. Like books, magazines, and newspapers, orders and opinions written by judges are more likely than not to take the form of digital images rather than tangible objects.

Indeed, with so much of today's writing embedded in the truncated protocols of social media and other "real time" forms of expression, the clarity and persuasive quality the authors of the first edition sought to teach are particularly important for judges' writing. But the elements of good writing are remarkably constant, and we think that you will find the principles explained so thoughtfully in the first edition no less applicable today.

Jeremy D. Fogel
Director, Federal Judicial Center

I. Introduction

Judicial opinions serve three functions. First, written opinions communicate a court's conclusions and the reasons for them to the parties and their lawyers. Second, when published, opinions announce the law to judges, academics, other lawyers, and the interested public. Finally, the preparation of a written opinion imposes intellectual discipline on the author, requiring the judge to clarify his or her reasoning and assess the sufficiency of precedential support for it.

The opinion should fairly, clearly, and accurately state the significant facts and relevant rules of law and demonstrate by its analysis the reasonableness of its conclusions. Misstating significant facts or authorities is a mark of carelessness, and it undermines the opinion's authority and integrity. Unclear or ambiguous writing reflects the author's lack of clear thinking and defeats the opinion's purpose.

This manual is intended to encourage judges and law clerks to think critically about their writing—not only about what to include and what to exclude, but also about how to write well. We expect that newly appointed judges and their law clerks will be the principal users of this manual. It therefore takes a functional approach to opinion writing: describing the considerations that arise at each stage of the writing and editing process; recommending organizational and stylistic techniques; and explaining the reasons for its recommendations. In keeping with the principle that there is no single right way to write an opinion, the manual explores alternatives and the considerations for choosing among them.

This manual should also help experienced judges take a fresh look at their approaches to writing and their styles. Professor Robert Leflar wrote:

> Pride of authorship is by no means an unmitigated evil. . . . [T]his pride can drive a man to hard work and with meticulous effort. The poorest opinions are apt to be written by judges who take no pride in them, who regard the preparation of them as mere chores. Pride in work well done is a proper incident of good craftsmanship in any field of work, including law. An opinion in which the author takes no pride is not likely to be much good.[1]

---

1. Robert Leflar, *Some Observations Concerning Judicial Opinions*, 61 Colum. L. Rev. 810, 813 (1961).

This manual is not intended to proclaim the right way of writing an opinion. Anyone who attempts to announce authoritative rules of good writing invites debate and comparison. As one judge said, "I have one overarching rule. That is, don't have any such rules." Indeed, in a leading text on good writing, E. B. White acknowledged that "[s]tyle rules of this sort are, of course, somewhat a matter of individual preference, and even the established rules of grammar are open to challenge."[2]

Instead, the purpose of the manual is to stimulate judges to think as systematically about writing their opinions as they do about deciding their cases. Judges should ask themselves: Am I writing this way because this is how I've always done it, or is there a better way? Is there a reason for organizing the opinion this way? For including these particular facts? For discussing this issue at length? For citing this case? Is this sentence clear? Are all the words in it necessary?

In the following parts, the manual takes readers through the opinion-writing process. Part 2 suggests issues to consider in deciding whether to write a formal opinion, a memorandum, or an unpublished opinion. Part 3 discusses steps a judge should take before starting to write. Part 4 discusses the organization and content of an opinion. Part 5 offers suggestions on language, style, and editing. Part 6 presents considerations for cowriting an opinion, commenting on the opinions of other members of the court, and writing dissenting and concurring opinions. Part 7 contains a list of books and articles that may be useful to those who want to read more about judicial writing. The appendices provide examples of some of the writings discussed in the manual, such as summary orders and dissenting opinions.

---

2. William Strunk, Jr., & E. B. White, The Elements of Style xvii (4th ed. 2000).

II. Determining the Scope of the Opinion

A judicial opinion informs parties of the outcome of their case and articulates the legal principles on which the decision is based in order to guide the bench, the bar, academia, and the public. Because written decisions serve both case-deciding and law-making functions, they range in form from one-sentence, unpublished summary orders to formally structured, citation-laden, full-dress opinions. An opinion that is intended only to inform the parties of the outcome of their dispute should not be as elaborate as one intended to serve as a precedent. Before beginning to write, judges should decide what purpose the opinion will serve and how to write it to suit that purpose.

Three types of decisions

This manual will refer to three types of written decisions: full-dress opinions, memorandum opinions, and summary orders.

Full-dress opinions are those that present a structured discussion of the facts, legal principles, and governing authorities involved in a case. The significance or number of the issues presented in a case, the novelty of the question it poses, and the complexity of the facts are among the factors that determine whether an opinion requires full-dress treatment.

Memorandum opinions are appropriate if the decision does not require a comprehensive, structured explanation but still needs some explanation of the rationale. They are generally brief and informal and may or may not be published. Per curiam opinions are generally included in this category. Appendix A contains an example of a memorandum opinion.

Summary orders simply state the disposition of the case. They sometimes include a brief statement of findings and conclusions, but often provide little or no explanation. Summary orders are usually unpublished. Appendix B contains an example of a summary order.

The next section discusses some of the factors a judge should consider in determining what kind of opinion to write.

Factors to consider

Three factors influence the scope and style of an opinion: the complexity of the facts and nature of the legal issues, the intended audience, and whether the opinion will be published. Although the manual addresses these factors separately, they are interrelated.

Facts and issues

The complexity of the facts and the nature of the legal issues are the principal factors that determine the kind of opinion required. If the precedents are clear and the material facts are not complicated, the scope of the opinion will be limited. If the controlling law is uncertain or the material facts are complex, exposition and analysis are needed to explain the reasons for the court's decision. Some cases that present complex fact patterns may require lengthy discussion of the facts even though the applicable law may be simple. Other cases that raise novel legal issues may require extended analysis of law and policy.

The scope of an opinion will be influenced by how well developed the law is on the matter at issue. Judges should consider whether the issue has previously been decided authoritatively and whether another opinion would aid in the development or explanation of the law. If the issue has been thoroughly discussed in prior opinions, the judge need not trace the origins of the law or elaborate on its interpretation. In some cases, it is sufficient to affirm a decision for the reasons stated by the court below. If the decision merely closes a gap in existing law, little more is needed than an explanation of the applicable principles and the reasons for the court's choice among them. If, however, the decision contributes to the development of the law, a brief, published per curiam or memorandum opinion is appropriate. A summary order may be sufficient if clear existing law is simply being applied to facts that are undisputed or that are made indisputable on appeal because, for example, they are jury findings supported by substantial evidence.

When, however, an opinion involves less developed areas of the law and lays down a new rule or modifies an old one, the judge must think not only about the decision's rationale but also about its impact as precedent. The judge should discuss and analyze the precedents in the area, the new direction the law is taking, and the effect of the decision on existing law. Even if it appears that the litigants do not need a detailed statement of the facts, the opinion should present sufficient facts to define for other readers the precedent it creates and to delineate its boundaries. The relevant precedents—and the relevant policies—should be analyzed in sufficient detail to establish the rationale for the holding.

Audience

Opinions are written primarily for the litigants and their lawyers, and for the lower courts or agencies whose decisions they review. If an opinion is addressed to the parties, it should provide them with a fair and accurate statement of what was before the court for decision, what the court decided, and what the reasons for the decision were. This can generally be accomplished without a full-dress opinion. The parties will be familiar with the facts and will generally not be interested in an extensive exploration of the law, other than what is needed to give the losing party a clear explanation for the result.

The judge must also ask whether the opinion has something to say to others besides the parties. Opinions intended to inform other audiences may require additional factual development and legal analysis. How much analysis is required, and how detailed it must be, depends on the subject matter and the probable audience. Judges may assume a certain level of familiarity with the law on the part of lawyers. But if a case involves an arcane area of law familiar primarily to specialists—tax, labor, or antitrust law, for example—a thorough discussion of the facts and legal background will be needed, and the judge should avoid the use of technical language and should define any technical terms that must be used.

An opinion remanding a case must tell the lower court what is expected on remand. An opinion that sets guidelines for trial courts to follow must state the factual basis, legal rationale, and policy foundation of the guidelines sufficiently so that trial judges can apply them correctly.

The judge needs to consider whether a statement of facts and legal analysis that adequately explain the decision to the parties will also enable a higher court to understand the basis for the decision. When the decision is based on complex facts, a more elaborate explanation than is necessary for the parties may be helpful to the appellate court. And when the decision involves novel issues or an emerging area of law, it is appropriate to trace the prior development of the law and to explain the legal and policy rationales at some length. Opinions should not, however, be turned into briefs or vehicles for advocacy.

Members of the general public will rarely read opinions. But reporters from the media will communicate what they believe to be the substance of an opinion that strikes them as being of public interest. When an opinion addresses an issue of general public interest or is likely to attract media attention, it should be written in a manner that will ensure it cannot be misunderstood. The mark of a well-written opinion is that it is comprehensible to an intelligent layperson.

Publication

The courts of appeals have adopted rules, internal operating procedures, and other policies concerning publication and non-publication of opinions. Some of the policies specify criteria for determining whether an opinion should be published. For example, D.C. Circuit Rule 36(c)(2) establishes the following publication criteria:

> An opinion, memorandum, or other statement explaining the basis for this court's action in issuing an order or judgment will be published if it meets one or more of the following criteria:
>
> (A) with regard to a substantial issue it resolves, it is a case of first impression or the first case to present the issue in this court;
>
> (B) it alters, modifies, or significantly clarifies a rule of law previously announced by the court;
>
> (C) it calls attention to an existing rule of law that appears to have been generally overlooked;
>
> (D) it criticizes or questions existing law;
>
> (E) it resolves an apparent conflict in decisions within the circuit or creates a conflict with another circuit;
>
> (F) it reverses a published agency or district court decision, or affirms a decision of the district court upon grounds different from those set forth in the district court's published opinion;
>
> (G) it warrants publication in light of other factors that give it general public interest.

Similar criteria are included in First Circuit Rule 36(b)(1); Fourth Circuit Rule 36(a); Fifth Circuit Rule 47.5.1; Sixth Circuit Internal Operating Procedure 32.1(b); Ninth Circuit Rule 36-2; and Federal Circuit Internal Operating Procedure 10.

Other circuits have more general guidelines, giving judges latitude to decide whether to publish opinions. The Third Circuit, for example, has "two forms of opinions: precedential and not precedential," and "[p]recedential opinions are posted on the court's internet website."[3] The Second Circuit permits disposition by summary order "[w]hen a decision in a case is unanimous and each panel judge believes that no jurisprudential purpose is served by an opinion . . . ."[4] Otherwise, written opinions, including per curiam opinions, are published.[5]

In the district courts, the decision to publish is entirely in the judge's discretion. (Note, however, that some legal publishers, including Westlaw, put certain district court orders and opinions on line whether or not the judge designates them for publication and even sometimes when a judge states that the order or opinion is "not for publication" or "not to be cited." The publishers base their decision on whether they think that the order or opinion is significant or otherwise of interest.) Because decisions of district judges are merely persuasive authority—that is, they are not binding precedent even in their own districts—publication of such decisions should be the exception. In addition, time constraints argue against writing formal opinions unless the decision involves a novel or complex issue or a matter of public importance and thus may be useful to attorneys and judges or be of interest to the public.

Because unpublished decisions are written primarily for the parties, they will require little or no elaboration of the facts and law. Often they will take the form of summary orders or memorandum opinions. The determination as to whether a disposition should be published or unpublished should be made as soon as possible, so that the judge who writes the opinion will not spend an undue amount of time on it if publication is not warranted.

---

3. 3d Cir. I.O.P. ch. 5.1, 5.2. *See also* 7th Cir. R. 32.1 ("It is the policy of the circuit to avoid issuing unnecessary opinions"); 8th Cir. I.O.P. IV.B ("The panel determines whether the opinion . . . is to be published or unpublished"); 11th Cir. I.O.P. 6 ("Opinions that the panel believes to have no precedential value are not published").

4. 2d Cir. I.O.P. 32.1.1.

5. *See also* 10th Cir. R. 36.1 (permitting disposition without opinion when "the case does not require application of new points of law that would make the decision a valuable precedent").

III. Preparing to Write the Opinion

Before beginning to write an opinion, judges should think through what they want to say and how they want to say it. They should consider the scope of the opinion, the prospective audience, and whether the opinion will be published. They should marshal the material facts, identify the issues and the applicable rules of law, and determine the appropriate form of judicial relief. In short, they must break the case down into its components. A judge should have reached a decision—if only a tentative one—before beginning to write an opinion. Setting down the reasons in writing then constitutes the process of justifying the decision. As Judge Ruggero Aldisert wrote, "If a judge wants to write clearly and cogently, with words parading before the reader in logical order, the judge must first think clearly and cogently, with thoughts laid out in neat rows."[6]

This does not mean that judges will not change their minds after they have started to write. Sometimes judges may decide in advance where they want to go, but in the process of writing discover that they cannot get there. Justice Roger Traynor wrote that he

> found [no] better test for the solution of a case than its articulation in writing, which is thinking at its hardest. A judge, inevitably preoccupied with the far-reaching effect of an immediate solution as a precedent, often discovers that his tentative views will not jell in the writing. He wrestles with the devil more than once to set forth a sound opinion that will be sufficient unto more than the day.[7]

Nevertheless, the writing should reflect only the final decision and the reasons for it. If the decision is a close one, the opinion should say so, but it should not record every step and misstep the writer took along the way.

Developing outlines

Outlines help to organize a writer's thoughts. For judicial writing, they may take a variety of forms:

---

6. Ruggero J. Aldisert, Opinion Writing 11 (2d ed. 2009).
7. Roger Traynor, *Some Open Questions on the Work of State Appellate Courts*, 24 U. Chi. L. Rev. 211, 218 (1957).

- a formal, written outline prepared by the judge or a law clerk;
- a rough sketch of important facts, issues, and points to discuss;
- a bench memorandum prepared by a law clerk in advance of oral argument, which the judge has marked up after the argument and conference;
- a brief checklist; or
- perhaps only an unwritten mental framework.

Whatever the outline's form, the point is that judges, like all other good writers, must organize their thoughts before starting to write.

A good time to prepare an outline is shortly after the conference at which the case is discussed and the opinion assigned, when the judge's own ideas and those of the other judges are fresh in mind. The outline can then also serve as an informal record of the discussion at the conference.

Using law clerks

Law clerks can provide substantial assistance to the judge faced with writing an opinion. Discussions with law clerks are helpful in planning the opinion and developing the outline. The opportunity to test one's thoughts in vigorous exchanges with the clerks throughout the opinion-writing process is invaluable. The judge and the law clerks can discuss and criticize the opinion as it develops, ferret out error and ambiguity, and polish the final product.

In the writing process itself, judges use their law clerks in different ways. Some limit the clerk's work to performing research; preparing bench memos; and editing, cite-checking, and commenting on the judge's drafts. Some assign the writing of the first draft to a law clerk in routine cases only; others have clerks write first drafts in even the most complex cases, having found that working from a draft makes the task of writing the opinion easier. A clerk assigned to write the first draft should use an outline developed by or with the judge, and should understand the scope, organization, and probable outcome of the opinion.

Many judges, having found that it takes more time to work with a clerk's draft, write their own draft, then polish it into the final product. Some judges invite the law clerk to rewrite the judge's first draft before the judge returns to it for preparation of the final version. Working with electronic documents facilitates this give-and-take between judges and law clerks in drafting opinions.

The process the judge uses depends on his or her own work habits and style and on the capabilities of the law clerk. The judge must always remember, however, that the law clerk usually is fresh out of law school and has little practical experience. Even a distinguished academic record does not qualify a law clerk to practice the craft of judging, to draw the fine line between reversible and harmless error, to make the sometimes delicate assessment of the effect of precedent, or to recognize subtle distinctions in the applicable law. It is the unusual law clerk who has perfected a writing style that makes for a satisfactory opinion. Law clerks' fact statements, analysis, and conclusions may require major revisions. Judges should not simply edit draft opinions. No matter how capable the clerk, the opinion must always be the judge's work.

Reviewing materials

Little need be said about the materials to review. The judge will, of course, have the briefs of the parties and the law clerk's bench memorandum. When an opinion turns on the specifics of testimony or on what occurred in the courtroom, there may be no substitute for reading the relevant portions of the transcript; rarely will excerpts or summaries in briefs convey the significance of these events fairly and fully. If an exhibit is crucial, it should be examined. Reference to the record may also be necessary to determine the precise procedural course by which an appeal has reached the court and the relevant proceedings below. The judge will therefore want to have access to the record while preparing the opinion. Listening to an audio recording of oral argument, if one is available, can help refresh the judge's memory of the significant issues and the arguments made.

IV. Writing the Opinion

A judicial opinion should identify the issues presented, set out the relevant facts, and apply the governing law to produce a clear, well-reasoned decision of the issues that must be resolved. The guidelines that follow are intended to help judges write opinions that will meet these requirements.

Structure

A full-dress opinion should contain five elements:
1. an introductory statement of the nature, procedural posture, and result of the case;
2. a statement of the issues to be decided;
3. a statement of the material facts;
4. a discussion of the governing legal principles and resolution of the issues; and
5. the disposition and necessary instructions.

The organization and style of opinions will, of course, vary from case to case, but this is the framework on which to build.

Clear and logical organization of the opinion will help the reader understand it. The use of headings and subheadings or Roman numerals, or other means of disclosing the organization to the reader, is always helpful, particularly when the opinion is long and the subject matter complex. Headings, subheadings, and subdivisions not only provide road signs for the reader, they also help the writer organize his or her thoughts and test the logic of the opinion. They also enable a judge who wishes not to join some part of the opinion to identify it. And they assist in the indexing and classification of opinions and their retrieval by researchers.

The following sections discuss each of the elements of an opinion.

Introduction

The purpose of the Introduction is to orient the reader to the case. It should state briefly what the case is about, the legal subject matter, and the result. It may also cover some or all of the following:
1. *The parties:* The parties should be identified, if not in the Introduction, then early in the opinion, preferably by name, and

names should be used consistently throughout. (The use of legal descriptions, such as "appellant" and "appellee," tends to be confusing, especially in multi-party cases.)
2. *The procedural and jurisdictional status:* The basis for jurisdiction, relevant prior proceedings, and how the case got before the court should be outlined.
3. *The issue:* The issue or issues to be decided should be identified, unless they are so complex that they are better treated in a separate section.

Summarizing the holding at the outset can save time for readers, particularly researchers who will be able to determine immediately whether to read the rest of the opinion. Providing a terse summary of the holding at the start of the opinion also helps the judge state it precisely and succinctly. The final version of the Introduction may be best written after the opinion is completed, when the judge has refined the issues, the conclusions, and the supporting analysis.

Some judges prefer to place the holding at the end, believing that an opinion will be more persuasive if the reader must read through it before learning the outcome.

Statement of issues

The statement of issues is the cornerstone of the opinion; how the issues are formulated determines which facts are material and what legal principles govern. Judges should not be bound by the attorneys' analyses; they should state the issues as they see them, even if this differs from how the lawyers state them. That an issue has been raised by the parties does not mean that it must be addressed in the opinion if it is not material to the outcome of the case.

The statement of issues should be brief. Although an issue or two can often be sufficiently identified in the Introduction, the number or complexity of the issues in some cases may require separate sections.

The statement of issues may come before or after the statement of facts. Stating the issues first will make the fact statement more meaningful to the reader and help focus on material facts. In some cases, however, it may be difficult to state the issues clearly unless the reader is familiar with the material facts. This may be true, for example, when the issue is procedural and requires an explanation of the context.

The statement of issues should not be confused with recitals of the parties' contentions. Lengthy statements of the parties' contentions, occasionally found in opinions, are not a substitute for analysis and reasoning, and they should be avoided.

Statement of facts

In a single-issue case, the facts can be set forth in one statement early in the opinion. But when a case raises a series of issues, some facts may not be relevant to all of the issues. This situation confronts the judge with the difficult task of presenting enough facts at the outset to make the opinion understandable without later repeating facts when discussing particular issues that require further elaboration. In such a case, the initial statement of facts can be limited to necessary historical background, and the specific decisional facts can be incorporated in the analysis of the issues they concern.

Only the facts that are necessary to explain the decision should be included, but what is necessary to explain the decision is not always obvious and may also vary depending on the audience. An unpublished memorandum opinion intended only for the parties does not require background or historical facts; the opinion need only identify the facts that support the conclusion. However, background facts may sometimes be helpful in giving the context of a decision and explaining its rationale. And opinions that are likely to be read by audiences other than the parties may require lengthier fact statements to provide the context for the decision and delineate its scope.

Excessive factual detail can be distracting. Dates, for example, tend to confuse readers and should not be included unless they are material to the decision or helpful to its understanding. Although brevity and simplicity are always desirable, they are secondary to the need for a full and fair fact statement. Facts significant to the losing side should not be omitted.

Some judges like to include facts that, although not material to the decision, add color. "We've got to have some fun," one judge said. Some feel that this is a mark of the author's flair and improves readability. There is the obvious danger, however, that the reader may think the decision is based on these facts even though they are not material. Moreover, colorful writing—though appealing to the author—may be seen by the parties as trivializing the case. It must therefore be used with caution.

Above all, the statement of facts must be accurate. The judge should not assume that the facts recited in the parties' briefs are stated correctly. There is no substitute for checking fact references against the record. No matter how good the lawyers are, the judge may find that the way facts are stated in the record differs from the way they are stated in the briefs. If time does not permit the judge to read the entire record, a law clerk should be assigned that task, with instructions to mark all the relevant parts for the judge to review.

Discussion of legal principles

The discussion of legal principles is the heart of the opinion. It must demonstrate that the court's conclusion is based on reason and logic. It should convince the reader of the correctness of the decision by the power of its reasoning, not by advocacy or argument. The judge must deal with arguably contrary authorities and opposing arguments, and must confront the issues squarely and deal with them forthrightly. Although the opinion need not address every case and contention, the discussion of legal principles must be sufficient to demonstrate to the losing party that the court has fully considered the essentials of its position.

The following guidelines apply to the discussion of legal principles.

Standard of review

The opinion should specify the controlling standard of review at the outset of the discussion of legal principles. Unless the reader is told whether review is under the de novo, the clearly erroneous, or the abuse of discretion standard, the meaning of the decision may be obscure. Moreover, specifying the standard of review helps the judge discipline the analysis.

Appendix C provides examples of clearly stated standards of review.

Order of discussion of issues

Just as the judge should not be wedded to counsel's formulation of the issues, he or she should not feel compelled to address the issues in the order in which counsel presented them. The order in which to address the issues will be dictated by the organization of the opinion. Generally, dispositive issues should be discussed first. The order in which those issues are taken up will be governed by the opinion's reasoning. If non-dispositive issues are addressed at all—for educational reasons or to guide further proceedings—the judge should discuss them near the end of the opinion.

Issues to address

As a general proposition, an opinion should address only the issues that need to be resolved to decide the case. If the court determines that an issue not raised by the parties is dispositive and should be addressed—even though the parties have not properly preserved and presented it—the court should notify counsel and provide them with the opportunity to brief it.

Issues not necessary to the decision but seriously raised by the losing party should be discussed only to the extent necessary to show that they have been considered. The line between what is necessary to the decision and what is not, however, is not always clear. Occasionally, a full explanation of the rationale for a decision may be enhanced by discussion of matters not strictly a part of the holding. Moreover, a judge may find it efficient to address issues not necessary to the decision if the judge can thereby provide useful guidance for the lower court on remand. However, judges must be careful not to decide issues that are not before them and to avoid advisory opinions and unnecessary expressions of views that may tie the court's hands in a future case.

Alternative holdings

Stating separate and independent grounds for a decision adds strength to the decision but diminishes its value as a precedent. Professor Bernard Witkin argues that judges should avoid such rulings.[8] Statements such as "even if the facts were otherwise" or "assuming arguendo that we had not concluded thus and so" undermine the authority of the holding. Witkin suggests either limiting the "even if" approach to opinions where doing so is necessary to achieve a majority decision or

---

8. *See* Bernard E. Witkin, Manual on Appellate Court Opinions § 81 (1977).

avoiding it completely by phrasing the opinion in such a manner that the alternative ground is disposed of first and the substantial ground of the opinion is stated last. But in opinions that are likely to have little impact as precedent, there is no reason why the court should not base its decision on alternative grounds, without giving one precedence over the other.

Case citations

Most points of law are adequately supported by citation of the latest decision on point in the court's circuit or the watershed case, if there is one. String citations and dissertations on the history of the legal principle add nothing when the matter is settled in the circuit. Judges should resist the temptation of trying to impress people with their (or their law clerks') erudition.

If there is no authority in the circuit, it is appropriate to cite authority on point from other circuits. If an opinion breaks new ground, however, the judge should marshal existing authority and analyze the evolution of the law sufficiently to support the new rule.

Secondary sources

Because law review articles, treatises and texts, and non-legal sources are not primary authorities, they should be cited sparingly and only to serve a purpose. That purpose may be to refer to a sound analysis that supports the reasoning of the opinion. Some authors are so well respected in their fields that, in the absence of a case on point, their word is persuasive. Occasionally, public documents or other published works will shed light on relevant historical or policy considerations.

Quotations

If something important to the opinion has been said well in an earlier case, quoting relevant language from the case can be more persuasive and informative than merely citing or paraphrasing it. The impact of a quote, however, is inversely proportional to its length. Judges should quote briefly, and only when the language makes an important point.

While quotes should be short, they must also be fair. They must be used in context and accurately reflect the tenor of their source.

Avoiding advocacy

Justifying a decision will sometimes require explaining why contrary arguments were rejected. In addressing the main contentions of the losing side, however, an opinion should not become an argument between the judge and the lawyers, other judges on the court, or the court below. If the losing side has raised substantial contentions, the opinion should explain why they were rejected. But the opinion need not refute the losing party's arguments point by point or adopt a contentious or adversarial tone.

An opinion can—and properly should—carry conviction without becoming a tract. Judges should put aside emotion and personal feelings, and avoid using adjectives and adverbs unless they convey information material to the decision.

Treatment of the court below

Appellate opinions can and should correct trial court errors and provide guidance on remand, but they need not attack a trial court's wisdom or judgment, or even its attitude in order to reverse its decision. Moreover, an appellate opinion should avoid unnecessary criticism of the trial court, such as for failing to consider authority or resting on improper motives.

Disposition and instructions

Disposition of a case—and the mandate to the lower court or agency, when that is a part of the disposition—is the most important part of the concluding paragraph. Appellate courts should not speak in riddles. Simply to remand a case "for further proceedings consistent with the opinion" may leave the court below at sea. Opinions must spell out clearly what the lower courts or agencies are expected to do, without trespassing on what remains entrusted to their discretion. Thus, even if an abuse of discretion is found, the appellate court's decision is on the law, and the lower court or agency on remand retains the authority to exercise its discretion properly.

Appendix D contains examples of dispositions that provide clear instructions to the lower court or agency.

Summary disposition may be appropriate in cases in which only the parties and their lawyers are interested in the result, the facts are not complex, and the precedents are clear. It may take the form of a one-sentence order or a brief memorandum (see Appendix B). The court should state its reason for making a summary disposition. When a summary disposition is pursuant to circuit or local rule, that rule should be cited.

V. Editing the Opinion

Problems in judicial writing

The judges who were interviewed for this manual identified the following as the major problems in judicial writing: wordiness, lack of precision and clarity, poor organization, cryptic analysis, and pomposity and humor.

Wordiness

Wordiness means not just using two words when one will do, but trying to convey too much information and covering too many issues. In trying to write authoritatively, some judges belabor the obvious in lengthy discussions of uncontroversial propositions. Often wordiness reflects the writer's failure (or inability) to separate the material from the immaterial and do the tedious work of editing.

Lack of precision and clarity

Precision and clarity are the main concerns of good writing. Some legal writers lack the ability to write simple, straightforward prose. Often this is the result of some lawyers' tendency to overgeneralize when they are not sure of a legal principle or of how to state it precisely; they finesse the difficulty with vague expression. To write with clarity and precision, the writer must know exactly what he or she wants to say and must say that and nothing else.

Precision in judicial writing is important because judges write for posterity. Once an opinion is filed, lawyers and others will read it with an eye to how they can use it to serve their particular purpose, no matter how different that may be from what the judge had in mind. Thus, it is important for judicial writers to think about how their words might be used and to write in a manner that will forestall their misuse.

Painstaking and thoughtful editing is essential for precise writing. This means going over the opinion, sentence by sentence, and asking: What do I mean to say here, and have I said it and no more?

Poor organization

Another problem in judicial writing is poor organization. A sound opinion is the reflection of a logical process of reasoning from premises through principles to conclusions. The framework in which that process takes place should be visible to the reader from the organization of the opinion. That organization will be a road map that enables the reader to follow the reasoning from the beginning to the end without getting lost.

Cryptic analysis

While brevity is desirable in an opinion, judges must elaborate their reasoning sufficiently so that the reader can follow it. An opinion that omits steps in the reasoning essential to understanding it will fail to serve its purposes.

Pomposity and humor

Judicial writing can be pompous. The judge must avoid pompous writing in an opinion, such as arcane or florid language, use of the imperial "we" (by a single district judge), or expressions of irrelevant erudition. Although the use of humor is sometimes rationalized as an antidote to pomposity, it works better in after-dinner speeches than in judicial opinions. In the latter, it may strike the litigants—who are not likely to see anything funny in the litigation—as a sign of judicial arrogance and lack of sensitivity. Although some judges seem to have succeeded in using humor in their opinions, it is a risk not to be taken lightly. Nor need it be taken at all, for writing can be made lively, forceful, and interesting by its clarity and logic.

Guidelines for good writing

The following guidelines are suggested to help writers of opinions recognize and avoid the problems discussed above: eliminate unnecessary words, be succinct and direct, and use plain English.

Eliminate unnecessary words

It is difficult to improve on Professor Strunk's injunction to omit needless words:

> Vigorous writing is concise. A sentence should contain no unnecessary words, a paragraph no unnecessary sentences, for the same reason that a drawing should have no unnecessary lines and

a machine no unnecessary parts. This requires not that the writer make all sentences short, or avoid all detail and treat subjects only in outline, but that every word tell.[9]

Be succinct and direct

Brevity promotes clarity. Writing that makes its point briefly is more likely to be understood than writing that is lengthy. Writing succinctly also forces the writer to think clearly and focus on what he or she is trying to say.

Judicial writing should be direct. Judicial writers should use simple, declarative sentences and short paragraphs most of the time, but vary sentence length and structure where necessary for emphasis or contrast. They should also use the active voice and avoid such constructions as "it is said," "it is argued," and "it is well founded." They should weed out gratuitous adjectives and eliminate unnecessary adverbs such as "clearly," "plainly," and "merely."

Use plain English

Even complex ideas can be expressed in simple language that the lay reader can understand. To express an idea in simple language requires that the writer understand the idea fully, enabling him or her to break it down into its essential components. For example, although electricity is a complex scientific phenomenon, it can be explained in terms laypersons understand. So can tax, antitrust, and patent law. Judges should avoid using clichés, hackneyed phrases ("as hereinabove set forth," for example), Latin expressions ("vel non," for example), and legal jargon. When using terms of art, judges should consider whether they are commonly understood by their audience or require plain English definitions. There is a place for the elegant word, but it should not be necessary for the reader to have a dictionary at hand while reading an opinion. As legal writing expert Bryan Garner has written:

> [N]ever assume that traditional legal expressions are legally necessary. As often as not they are scars left by the law's verbal elephantiasis, which only lately has started into remission. Use words and phrases that you know to be both precise and as widely

---

9. Strunk & White, *supra* note 2, at 23.

understood as possible. Rarely can you justify the little-known word on grounds that it is a term of art.[10]

Use of footnotes and citations

Footnotes

The purpose of a footnote is to convey information that would disrupt the flow of the opinion if included in the text. The first question a judge should ask about a prospective footnote is whether its content is appropriate for inclusion in the opinion. If it is not important enough to go into the text, the judge must have some justification for including it in the opinion at all. The use of footnotes can be appropriate to convey information that supports the language of the opinion but is not necessary to understand it, such as the text of a statute or material from the record. Footnotes can also be used to acknowledge and briefly dispose of tangential issues. Some judges place all citations in footnotes, leaving the text entirely for discussion. But footnotes should not be used simply as a repository for information that the judge wants to keep but does not know what to do with. Some judges, conscious of the tendency to overuse footnotes, have strived to eliminate or at least reduce the number of footnotes in their opinions.[11]

Citations

The leading legal citation manual is *The Bluebook: A Uniform System of Citation*.[12] Mastering the arcana of citation forms, however, is not a productive use of judges' or law clerks' time. The purpose of citations is to assist researchers in identifying and finding the sources; a form of citation that will serve that end is sufficient. Whatever form of citation is used, it should be used consistently to avoid confusion and the appearance of lack of craftsmanship and care. Some judges maintain personal citation forms or style manuals that reflect their preferences. Such forms and manuals promote consistency, help orient new clerks, and encourage careful preparation of opinions.

---

10. Bryan A. Garner, The Elements of Legal Style 193 (2d ed. 2002).
11. *See, e.g.*, Abner J. Mikva, *Goodbye to Footnotes*, 56 U. Colo. L. Rev. 647 (1985).
12. The Bluebook: A Uniform System of Citation (Columbia Law Review Ass'n et al. eds., 19th ed. 2010) [hereinafter The Bluebook].

Careful editing

Careful writers edit their work critically to clarify the ambiguities, eliminate the superfluous, smooth the transitions, and tighten the structure. This is not an easy task, because when reading their own writing, writers tend to read what they meant to write rather than what they actually wrote.

Judges must strive to be objective about their writing, to read every paragraph carefully, and not to skip over text because it is familiar. A judge who is editing his or her own work must always ask these questions: Have I said precisely what I intended to say? Is there a better way to say it? Does the thought flow clearly and logically? Will the reader understand it?

The following techniques should help judicial writers improve their editing skills.

Reread and revise

Editing an opinion involves striking needless words and unnecessary facts, rewriting unclear sentences, eliminating repetition, reorganizing, and making the opinion cleaner and sharper. "I spend a lot of time editing, clearing away my own and the clerks' underbrush," one judge said. "The underbrush may be valuable someplace or sometime, but not here and now." This process may take the judge through many drafts before a polished opinion emerges.

Electronic word processing software is a boon to writers and editors. It greatly speeds up the writing process and facilitates editing and revising. But proofreading text on a computer screen is demanding, and without careful and repeated checking of a printed copy, typographical and other errors can be easily missed, even if automated spelling and grammar features are used.

In editing their opinions, judges should not focus solely on language, grammar, and style. They must also

- check for internal consistency;
- go back to the Introduction to see whether the opinion has addressed all of the issues and answered the questions as they were initially formulated;
- reread the statement of facts to see whether it covers all the facts significant to the decision and no more;

- review the legal discussion to see whether the opinion has addressed in logical order the issues that need to be addressed; and
- consider whether the Conclusion follows from the discussion.

Put the draft aside and come back to it with a fresh perspective

Judges can improve the editing process by "let[ting] the draft sit for a while and simmer," as one judge said. Although time constraints and mounting caseloads may make it difficult, delaying editing the opinion for even a few days may help the judge review things more objectively, gain new insights, and think of new ideas.

Ask a new reader to criticize a draft

A law clerk who has not worked on the opinion can serve a useful function by reading the draft with a fresh eye and offering editorial and substantive criticism. Even law clerks who have assisted the judge with the opinion can provide an editorial perspective that will help improve the finished product.

VI. Writing Joint Opinions, Dissents, and Concurrences

Appellate opinions represent the collective decision of several judges. The judge who writes the opinion must take into account the thinking of the other judges on the panel or en banc court and incorporate it into the opinion's rationale. Sometimes several judges participate in preparing an opinion, for example, when an opinion is written jointly or when judges comment on drafts prepared by the judge assigned to write the opinion. When the opinion does not represent the thinking of all of the members of the court, some judges may choose to prepare concurring or dissenting opinions. This part discusses some of the collegial considerations in opinion writing.

Joint opinions

In some circuits, the complexity and number of issues involved in a single case have resulted in jointly written opinions. Sometimes the opinion is designated as per curiam; at other times the authors of the different sections are identified. The review of long and technical administrative records in the D.C. Circuit, for example, has resulted in joint opinions.[13]

When a panel chooses to issue a joint opinion, considerable planning and coordination by both judges and law clerks are necessary to ensure a readable and coherent final opinion. It is desirable for the judges to hold a longer-than-usual post-argument conference to discuss the assignment of opinion sections, their interdependence, and joint assumptions or factual predicates. The panel may need to determine the sequence of sections to avoid confusion and repetition of basic facts or legal analyses.

Generally, one judge on the panel must assume coordinating authority and circulate an outline and summary of the proposed sections before writing begins. One judge, usually the coordinating judge, must also take responsibility for writing the Introduction and Conclusion, which cover all sections. The Introduction is usually brief

---

13. *See, e.g.*, Nat'l Wildlife Fed'n v. Hodel, 839 F.2d 694 (D.C. Cir. 1988); Ohio v. U.S. Dep't of Interior, 880 F.2d 432 (D.C. Cir. 1989). *See also* Chem. Mfrs. Ass'n v. Envtl. Prot. Agency, 870 F.2d 177 (5th Cir. 1989).

and confined to a statement of the proceedings leading to the court challenge. The facts in detail are better presented as needed in the individual sections.

After the authors have drafted and approved the various sections, the coordinating judge should assume authority to make non-substantive changes to the draft to eliminate duplication or gross stylistic differences. The law clerks usually meet to decide on a uniform citation and heading format.

Commenting on a draft prepared by another judge

Judges circulate draft opinions to other judges on a panel or en banc court to ensure that the opinion reflects the rationale of the judges in the majority. When commenting on an opinion written by another judge, it is always appropriate to comment on the opinion's substance, but inappropriate to comment on matters of style. When the distinction between substance and style is fuzzy, judges' comments are appropriate if the matter in question seems to speak for the court and thus might send a message that does not represent the view of the other judges.

If, for example, the discussion of a substantive issue is not written clearly, the other judges should bring this to the attention of the writing judge. When a citation to a case or law review article may represent a rationale that is not adopted by other judges, they should express their disagreement to the writing judge. When, however, a reviewing judge objects to stylistic, grammatical, or language choices simply on the basis of personal preference, such objections are best left unexpressed. Nevertheless, although judges are not grading the work of their colleagues, it is helpful to point out minor matters, such as typographical errors, either by a note to the author or by a telephone call between law clerks.

Dissenting opinions

Dissenting opinions can serve useful functions in communicating important information to an opinion's audiences and furthering the growth of the law. They may help to encourage en banc or certiorari review and to isolate and refine the issues for further appeal. They may promote legislative action to correct possible shortcomings in the law. Dissenting opinions may also help to narrow the scope of a decision by pointing out the possible dangers of the position the majority has taken or by indicating to other judges and the bar the limits of a particular decision and its effect on similar cases in the future.

Dissenting opinions are written at a potential cost, however. A dissent that sounds strident or preachy may contribute to divisiveness and ill feelings in the court, may undermine the authority of the majority opinion and of the court as an institution, and may create confusion. Whether judges should dissent depends on the nature of the case and the principle at issue. Judges generally should not write dissenting opinions when the principle at issue is settled and the decision has little significance outside the specific case. Cases that involve emerging legal principles or statutory interpretation in areas that will affect future activities of the bar, the public, and the government are more likely to warrant dissenting opinions than cases of limited application. The issue should be significant enough that the judge's "fever is aroused," as one judge said, but the motivation for writing a dissent should be to further the development of the law rather than to vent personal feelings. Judges considering whether to dissent should ask themselves whether the likely benefits outweigh the potential costs.

If a judge decides that writing a dissent will serve a useful purpose, the judge should write it as carefully and responsibly as an opinion of the court. Rarely should a judge dissent without an opinion; doing so communicates no information to the opinion's readers. The dissenting opinion should focus on the critical principles and distinguish the dissenter's rationale from that of the majority. The dissenting judge should state the points of disagreement forcefully and effectively without engaging in argument or advocacy. A dissenting opinion should not simply slash at the majority opinion or its author. Personal attacks, offensive language, or a condescending tone should not be used, although some judges believe that expressing moral outrage and restrained indignation may sometimes be appropriate.

Appendix E contains examples of brief dissenting opinions that reflect a temperate, reasoned tone in expressing sincere disagreement with the majority.

Concurring opinions

Most of the considerations applicable to dissenting opinions also apply to concurrences. Concurring opinions are appropriate where they are intended to define with greater precision the scope of the majority opinion or otherwise inform the parties and other audiences of what the writer believes are important points. Thus, judges may issue concurrences when there are two argued grounds for a decision, the majority justifies its decision on one of those grounds, and other judges believe the alternative ground should be stated. Concurrences may also serve to indicate to parties in future cases how far the court is willing to go down a particular road. A judge should not write a concurring opinion simply to add a point of view or personal statement that does not further either the decisional or educational value of the majority opinion. In deciding whether to write a concurring opinion, the judge should ask the question: Am I writing this for myself or for the good of the court?

Judges should include in their concurring opinions a statement of reasons why they are concurring. The point is not to present an alternative opinion of the court, but to indicate the point of departure from the majority and to further define the contours of the majority opinion. Concurrences should also not rehash the facts and legal principles on which the majority based its decision, unless the judge has interpreted the facts and principles in a different way. The arguments should be principled, and the tone should be instructive but not pedantic.

Appendix F contains examples of useful and narrowly written concurring opinions.

VII. Reading About Writing

One of the judges we interviewed said, "I think judges should constantly read books on writing." A dictionary, a thesaurus, and *The Bluebook: A Uniform System of Citation*[14] are the basic writing aids judges should have at hand. Judges should also be familiar with manuals on style and grammar and refer to them when questions arise. Strunk & White's *The Elements of Style*[15] is clear and concise, and is considered by many authorities to be the leading guide on writing style. A copy of it should be in every chambers. Many judges and legal writing experts consider Bryan Garner to be the preeminent authority on legal writing style. He has written numerous books on the topic, including *The Elements of Legal Style*[16] and the more comprehensive *The Redbook: A Manual on Legal Style*.[17]

Some judges find that reading old opinions helps them to improve the clarity of their writing. "Sometimes I'll remember an opinion that I think was particularly good in terms of teaching the legal principles," one judge said. "The old opinion will become sort of a textbook for how to skin that cat."

Another judge said, "I always tell my clerks to go back and read some good authors to see how they write and then try to think about that when they are writing law." Another observed:

> I find the best tool for trying to keep your writing from being totally dull and hard to read is to read non-legal things. I think the more non-legal books you read, the more you pick up interesting popular terms having application to the law and the more you can stay away from legal jargon or the same tired old words. I find that reading outside of the law, sometimes a phrase will stick in your mind, sometimes a word, sometimes an image. Analogizing to non-legal situations can liven up your writing, as can introducing unexpected words and images.

This manual will not suggest what should be on a judge's non-legal reading list (although several judges suggested that Ernest Hemingway's lean style is an excellent model for legal writing). The following,

---

14. The Bluebook, *supra* note 12.
15. Strunk & White, *supra* note 2.
16. Bryan A. Garner, The Elements of Legal Style (2d ed. 2002).
17. Bryan A. Garner, The Redbook: A Manual on Legal Style (2d ed. 2006).

however, are books and articles on legal writing that will assist judges in preparing clear and concise opinions.

Books

Ruggero A. Aldisert, Opinion Writing (2d ed. 2009).
Bryan A. Garner, The Elements of Legal Style (2d ed. 2002).
Bryan A. Garner, The Redbook: A Manual on Legal Style (2d ed. 2006).
Joyce J. George, Judicial Opinion Writing Handbook (5th ed. 2007).
William D. Popkin, Evolution of the Judicial Opinion: Institutional and Individual Styles (2007).
Bernard E. Witkin, Manual on Appellate Court Opinions (1977).
Richard C. Wydick, Plain English for Lawyers (5th ed. 2005).

Articles

Joseph Kimble, *The Straight Skinny on Better Judicial Opinions*, 9 Scribes J. Legal Writing 1 (2003–2004).
Robert A. Leflar, *Some Observations Concerning Judicial Opinions*, 61 Colum. L. Rev. 810 (1961).
Abner J. Mikva, *The Lester W. Roth Lecture: For Whom Judges Write*, 61 S. Cal. L. Rev. 1357 (1988).
Edward D. Re, Appellate Opinion Writing (Federal Judicial Center 1975).
Timothy P. Terrell, *Organizing Clear Opinions: Beyond Logic to Coherence and Character*, 38 Judges J. 4 (Spring 1999).
Irving Younger, *Bad Writing = Bad Thinking*, A.B.A. J. 90 (Jan. 1, 1987).

Appendix A: Sample Memorandum Opinion

The following excerpt is an example of a memorandum opinion.

This is a consolidated appeal from two actions . . . . Defendants . . . appeal from final judgments of foreclosure and sale entered in the [district court] dated . . . and . . . . We need not recite the facts of this case, since they are set forth in detail in the district court's two thorough opinions, reported at . . . . Familiarity with these facts is assumed. See also [related action].

The principal argument of [defendants] on appeal is this: The district court erred in dismissing the "faithless agent" defense to foreclosure under [state] law. That defense is an attempt to avoid the established rule of agency law that a principal is liable to third parties for the acts of an agent operating within the scope of the agent's real or apparent authority. *See British American & Eastern Co. v. Wirth Ltd.*, 592 F.2d 75, 80 (2d Cir. 1979). Appellants . . . do not contest that appellee . . ., the mortgagee of the properties involved here, was a third party. Nor do they deny that [appellee] was dealing with their agent [land company] and that the latter was acting within the scope of its apparent authority. Nevertheless, they invoke the faithless agent defense, claiming that [appellee] should be barred from foreclosing because it was aware of the mismanagement of B . . ., who was acting as president of [the land company]. To support this view, they point to evidence that [appellee] believed that B's mismanagement was the root cause of the default.

We are not persuaded that the district court erred in rejecting the faithless agent defense. Assuming arguendo that this defense may be invoked under the right circumstances, we considered and rejected it in [citation]. Indeed, the party asserting the faithless agent defense in [citation] appears to have been essentially the same, in all but name, as [defendants]. [Citation.] Moreover, even if, as defendants contend, principles of collateral estoppel do not bar their claim, we find the reasoning of the [citation] panel dispositive on this record. "It cannot be that a mortgagee's awareness of defaults under a mortgage constitutes awareness that a managing agent is engaged in self-dealing." [Citation.] On the record before us, "[f]aced with only conclusory allegations and unsupported factual assertions," we reject, as did the [citation] panel, the "'faithless agent' defense." [Citation.] The judgments of the district court are affirmed.

Appendix B: Sample Summary Order

The following is an example of a summary order.

This cause came to be heard on the transcript of record from the United States District Court for the District of _____ and was taken under submission.
1. Plaintiff... appeals pro se from an order dated December 21, 1989 of the United States District Court for the District of _____ denying appellant's motion for reconsideration of the district court's order of October 12, 1989, which granted the cross-motion for summary judgment of defendants-appellees .... This civil rights case arises out of appellees' failure to hire appellant for a position at the Veterans Administration Medical Center in ....
2. Appellant's principal claims on appeal appear to be that the district court abused its discretion, misinterpreted the facts in this case, misapplied various laws and misinterpreted Congress's intent in enacting Title VII of the Civil Rights Act of 1964.
3. We have carefully examined all of appellant's claims, and they are without merit. We affirm substantially for the reasons stated in the thorough opinions of... dated October 12, 1989 and December 21, 1989.
4. The order of the district court is affirmed.

Appendix C: Sample Standards of Review

The following are examples of clearly stated standards of review.

We review a district court's denial of a motion for a new trial for an abuse of discretion. *Robins v. Harum*, 773 F.2d 1004, 1006 (9th Cir. 1985). The reviewing court must consider whether the decision of the lower court "was based on a consideration of the relevant factors and whether there has been a clear error of judgment." *Citizens to Preserve Overton Park, Inc. v. Volpe*, 401 U.S. 402, 416, 91 S. Ct. 814, 823, 28 L. Ed. 2d 136 (1971).

* * *

Section 10(j) of the National Labor Relations Act, 29 U.S.C. § 160(j) (1982), authorizes district courts to grant interim injunctive relief to restore and preserve the status quo pending the Board's decision on the merits of an underlying unfair labor practice complaint. *E.g., Asseo v. Pan American Grain Co., Inc.*, 805 F.2d 23, 25 (1st Cir. 1986); *Fuchs v. Hood Industries, Inc.*, 590 F.2d 395, 397 (1st Cir. 1979). Under this statutory scheme, the district court is limited to the determination of (1) whether there is reasonable cause to believe that a violation of the Act, as alleged, has been committed, and (2) whether injunctive relief is appropriate under the circumstances. *Asseo*, 805 F.2d at 25; *Maram v. Universidad Interamericana de Puerto Rico*, 722 F.2d 953, 959 (1st Cir. 1983).

As we have previously stated, on appeal, this court's review is:

> limited to [determining] whether the district court was clearly erroneous in finding reasonable cause to believe that there were unfair labor practices and whether it abused its discretion in granting injunctive relief. *Union de Tronquistas de Puerto Rico v. Arlook*, 586 F.2d 872, 876 (1st Cir. 1978).

Asseo, 805 F.2d at 25. With these standards firmly in mind, we turn now to the merits of the appeal.

* * *

In reviewing findings by bankruptcy courts, we and the district courts may only reverse factual findings where we determine that they are clearly erroneous. *In re Killebrew*, 888 F.2d 1516, 1519 (5th Cir. 1989). Legal determinations, of course, we review de novo. *In re Comp-*

ton, 891 F.2d 1180, 1183 (5th Cir. 1990). As this appeal hinges upon whether [the debtor] intentionally deceived [the creditor]—a factual determination—we apply the clearly erroneous standard. *Cf. In re Rubin,* 875 F.2d 755, 758 (9th Cir. 1989).

Appendix D: Sample Dispositions

The following are examples of good, instructive dispositions.

We therefore grant the petition for review and order the [agency] not to initiate further prosecutions under the Penalty Rules until the agency has engaged in further rulemaking in accord with section 553. Nonetheless, pursuant to our remedial powers, we hold that the [agency] is free to hold pending cases in abeyance and resume prosecution upon the repromulgation of a scheme for adjudicating administrative civil penalty actions under section 1475.

* * *

For the foregoing reasons we will reverse the order of _____, dismissing this action and will remand the case to the district court to reinstate this action. On remand the district court should consider the preemption argument on the merits unless it upholds another defense to this action.

* * *

For the reasons stated, we order the district court to do the following: (1) The court will reconsider its order in respect to VOC cleanup; it will amend that order to require [defendant] to clean up VOCs in the soil at the . . . site to a level that it determines "public health" and the "public interest" require. (2) The court will reconsider the matter of "indirect costs," explaining, as we have set forth above, any denial of those costs as a sanction. In all other respects the judgment of the district court is affirmed.

Appendix E: Sample Brief Dissenting Opinions

The following are examples of brief dissenting opinions.

The reasons why I am constrained to dissent may be briefly stated.

The question whether an anti-takeover provision provides a "special protection" to debenture holders cannot be answered in the negative merely because the "Independent Directors" decided to waive their provisions and approve a particular transaction. These directors were explicitly empowered to act in this fashion by virtue of the fully disclosed terms of the provision. A significant function of an anti-takeover provision is to serve as a deterrent to hostile takeovers, including takeovers which would be contrary to the interests of both shareholders and debenture holders. One cannot, I believe, fairly characterize such a provision as being "worthless" to the debenture holders, even though as a matter of Delaware law directors owe a fiduciary duty solely to shareholders. The anti-takeover provision was therefore a "special protection" to debenture holders, albeit a limited one.

Federal securities laws do not impose an obligation to advise investors of the fundamentals of corporate governance. The disclosure required by the federal securities laws is not a "rite of confession or exercise in common law pleading. What is required is the disclosure of material objective factual matters." *Data Probe Acquisition Corp. v. Data Lab, Inc.*, 722 F.2d 1, 5–6 (2d Cir. 1983), *cert. denied*, 465 U.S. 1052, 104 S. Ct. 1326, 79 L. Ed. 722 (1984). Especially is this so where, as here, the investor complainants are sophisticated financial institutions making major investments. The role of the federal securities laws is not to remedy all perceived injustices in securities transactions. Rather, as invoked in this case, it proscribes only the making of false and misleading statements or material omissions.

Whether the Independent Directors breached an implied duty of good faith or otherwise acted contrary to their fiduciary obligations are matters of state law. Here, the federal claims were asserted only conditionally, the express condition being the failure of the state law claims. These state claims were properly dismissed by the court below for lack of pendent jurisdiction.

Believing no valid federal claim to be present, I would affirm essentially for the reasons set forth in the Opinions of the Magistrate and District Court.

* * *

In many respects this case represents good police work. It is clear, however, that defendants were of abnormally low intelligence and that *Miranda* warnings were not given. Even though appellants had not been taken in custody, it is also true they had not been furnished counsel or waived same. As the district court held, the government agents should have taken further precautions to ensure that [defendants] understood the situation and their rights. *See Henry v. Dees,* 658 F.2d 406, 411 (5th Cir. 1981).

Appendix F: Sample Brief Concurring Opinions

The following are examples of brief, narrowly written concurring opinions.

    I concur with most of Judge _____'s thoughtful discussion of the issues in this case. I am fully in accord with Part IIA and C and the rationale with respect to the claims against [defendant] and the state law claims. I agree also with the statement in Part IIB that "[d]ue process concerns are clearly not implicated in [defendants'] actions with regard to the letter from . . . ." I agree further that there is "no support . . . for plaintiff's fanciful conspiracy theory."

    I find no necessity, however, to adopt the statement quoted from *Rice v. Ohio Department of Transportation*, 887 F.2d 716, 719 (6th Cir. 1989), which may be interpreted to mean that the doctrine of *Will v. Michigan Department of State Police*, 491 U.S. 58 (1989), somehow bars suits under § 1983 against state officials when those officials are being sued in their individual capacities. I do not view *Will* as barring § 1983 suits against state officials whenever the suits concern actions taken in their individual capacities. Instead, I believe that *Will* bars suits against state officials only when those officials are sued in their official capacities.

    Accordingly, I would affirm the decision of the district court that under the facts of this case defendants . . . enjoy qualified immunity.

* * *

    I concur with the results reached by Judge _____ and in his opinion except as to his analysis of the First Amendment issue. For the reasons stated in my concurring opinion in [citation], I believe the . . . regulations are permissible time, place, and manner restrictions on speech in the [plaintiff's] profession.

The Federal Judicial Center

Board
The Chief Justice of the United States, *Chair*
Judge Catherine C. Blake, U.S. District Court for the District of Maryland
Magistrate Judge Jonathan W. Feldman, U.S. District Court for the Western District of New York
Judge James F. Holderman, Jr., U.S. District Court for the Northern District of Illinois
Judge Michael M. Melloy, U.S. Court of Appeals for the Eighth Circuit
Chief Judge C. Ray Mullins, U.S. Bankruptcy Court for the Northern District of Georgia
Judge Edward C. Prado, U.S. Court of Appeals for the Fifth Circuit
Judge Kathryn H. Vratil, U.S. District Court for the District of Kansas
Judge Thomas F. Hogan, Director of the Administrative Office of the U.S. Courts

Director
Judge Jeremy D. Fogel

Deputy Director
John S. Cooke

About the Federal Judicial Center
The Federal Judicial Center is the research and education agency of the federal judicial system. It was established by Congress in 1967 (28 U.S.C. §§ 620–629), on the recommendation of the Judicial Conference of the United States.

By statute, the Chief Justice of the United States chairs the Center's Board, which also includes the director of the Administrative Office of the U.S. Courts and seven judges elected by the Judicial Conference.

The organization of the Center reflects its primary statutory mandates. The Education Division plans and produces education and training programs for judges and court staff, including video programs, publications, curriculum packages for in-court training, and Web-based programs and resources. The Research Division examines and evaluates current and alternative federal court practices and policies. This research assists Judicial Conference committees, who request most Center research, in developing policy recommendations. The Center's research also contributes substantially to its educational programs. The two divisions work closely with two units of the Director's Office—the Information Technology Office and the Communications Policy & Design Office—in using print, broadcast, and on-line media to deliver education and training and to disseminate the results of Center research. The Federal Judicial History Office helps courts and others study and preserve federal judicial history. The International Judicial Relations Office provides information to judicial and legal officials from foreign countries and assesses how to inform federal judicial personnel of developments in international law and other court systems that may affect their work.

www.ingramcontent.com/pod-product-compliance
Lightning Source LLC
Chambersburg PA
CBHW070408190526
45169CB00003B/1162